T0198904

An Illustrated Explanation of Earthed Equipotential Bonding

D.W. Cockburn

www.illustrationexplains.com

AuthorHouse™ UK
1663 Liberty Drive
Bloomington, IN 47403 USA
www.authorhouse.co.uk
UK TFN: 0800 0148641 (Toll Free inside the UK)
UK Local: 02036 956322 (+44 20 3695 6322 from outside the UK)

Because of the dynamic nature of the Internet, any web addresses or links contained in this book may have changed
since publication and may no longer be valid. The views expressed in this work are solely those of the author and do not
necessarily reflect the views of the publisher, and the publisher hereby disclaims any responsibility for them.

Any people depicted in stock imagery provided by Getty Images are models,
and such images are being used for illustrative purposes only.
Certain stock imagery © Getty Images.

This book is printed on acid-free paper.

ISBN: 978-1-4490-4161-8 (sc)

Library of Congress Control Number: 2011960284

Print information available on the last page.

Published by AuthorHouse 11/24/2020

authorHOUSE®

"In seeking to protect the most vulnerable to 230v,
we end up protecting ourselves from 400v…"

Terminology and Definitions:

Terminology and definitions on this subject tend to vary from one generation to another, which can have the affect of distorting perceptions. Therefore I have chosen to re-use some of the older available terminology as this is the best way that I can see of explaining (and therefore hopefully understanding) what can otherwise appear to be a very complicated subject, the reason that this works is because using all of the available terminology as it is defined below demonstrates a coherent approach to providing a descriptive term for each and every situation and/or set of relevant circumstances.

Equipotential: – as close to 'equal potential' as it is reasonably practicable to achieve.

Earth leakage current: – current that regularly flows at a safe potential difference (voltage) from current using equipment to earth within a healthy system.

Earth fault current: – current that flows at a dangerous potential difference (voltage) from faulty current using equipment or from damaged circuit conductors to earth, which in a healthy system is only allowed to flow for a controlled (and therefore safe) period of time before causing automatic disconnection of the supply.

Direct contact: – coming into contact with an energised circuit conductor.
(This can occur as a result of a failure in 'Basic protection').

Direct contact under fault conditions: – coming into contact with a conductor that has its' self become and remained 'hazardous live' as a result of coming into contact with an energised circuit conductor.
(This can occur as a result of a failure in 'Fault protection').
Please note: Within a healthy system 'Direct contact under fault conditions' is easily prevented, prevention is achieved with the use of 'earthed equipotential bonding and automatic disconnection of supply' in conjunction with effective over-current protection (which prevents the cabling being worn out too quickly through being over-heated); and regular 'insulation resistance testing' of circuit conductors (which is used to identify circuit conductors that are becoming worn out before they can present a danger).

Indirect contact: – coming into contact with an earthed conductor, whilst 'earth leakage current' is flowing through the earthing system.

Indirect contact under fault conditions: – coming into contact with an earthed conductor, whilst 'earth fault current' is flowing through the earthing system.

Circuit conductor: – any conductor in a system which is intended to carry electric current in normal conditions, or to be energised in normal conditions, but <u>does not</u> include a conductor provided solely to perform a protective function by connection to earth.

Conductor: – any conductor of electrical energy (including; 'circuit protective', 'equipotential bonding' and 'supplementary equipotential bonding' conductors).

Introduction:

Either by luck or by judgement, flexible cables that we use everyday are something that it is very difficult for the human hand to get a firm grip of.

If a person should inadvertently pick up a damaged, 'hazardous live' flex or extension lead, we 'hope' that the flex or extension lead will be pulled through or out of the hand and as a result, contact with the 'hazardous live' circuit conductor will be broken.

Therefore coming into contact with a 'hazardous live' flex or extension lead will, regardless of the protective device used cause current to flow in varying 'magnitudes', into the human body. But as the resistance through the human body to earth, is 'constantly variable' (see neon-screwdriver), limiting the 'duration' of any resultant electric shock passing through the human body, remains in many instances reliant on the victims' ability to let go of the 'hazardous live' flex or extension lead!

One of the objectives of 'earthed equipotential bonding and automatic disconnection of supply', or EEBADS as its' known, is to limit the 'duration' of an electric shock, resulting from a 'hazardous live' circuit conductor such as a damaged flex or extension lead, coming into contact with another piece of conductive material such as a piece of 'exposed metalwork' which also becomes 'hazardous live' as a result but unlike the flex, may be firmly gripped by the human hand.

This book is intended to explain in the form of simplified illustrations, why it is important to create a 'low resistance' continuous path, from all of the exposed conductive elements within a building, to an electrical safety 'earth'.

In order for current to flow 'through' the human body, the body will need to have a second point of contact, usually with earth but sometimes with neutral or worse, with a 'hazardous live' conductor supplied by a different 'phase'!

Let us first concentrate on the human body's resistance to 'earth':

In order to understand more easily, we can experiment for ourselves by employing the humble 'neon screwdriver'.

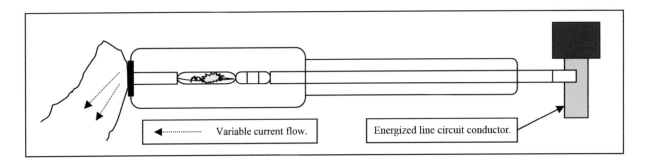

Variable current flow.

Energized line circuit conductor.

The 'neon screwdriver' is not recommended for use when verifying whether or not a circuit is energized, this is because they are notoriously un-reliable. But for our purposes they are a 'Godsend', as they demonstrate perfectly the constantly variable nature of the resistance through the human body to earth.

Try to use your 'neon screwdriver' on a hot dry afternoon, while wearing a sturdy pair of site boots and it may hardly even flicker. But then try pressing your knee against a wall and you may well see it flicker into life.

Try using one in Australia or in Southern Europe and it will probably never work at all, but try wearing 'kicked out trainers' and using one on a misty morning in a Welsh Valley and it will be as bright as a new pin, even upstairs!

Once you have tried using a 'neon screwdriver' in enough different circumstances, you will soon come to the conclusion that living in the British Isles at least, the human body is more or less constantly in contact with earth to some degree.

Please note:
The 'residual current devices' that are currently used to automatically disconnect electrical circuits, rely on measuring the amount of current imbalance between line and neutral in any given circuit. In order that enough current imbalance occurs to disconnect the circuit, a sufficient amount of earth fault current must escape back to earth within a very short space of time.

When the human body is stood in bare feet on wet grass, or when the human body is in contact with an earthed exposed-conductive-part or extraneous-conductive-part, earth fault current will be able to flow quickly enough through the body, for a 'residual current device' to be effective.

When the human body is in contact with neither of these, the resistance of the human body to earth becomes 'constantly variable' to a degree where we can lose control of the speed of automatic disconnection of supply!

When we refer to 'earthed equipotential bonding' we are, basically talking about completing a circuit (or 'loop') between line and earth.

In order to simplify things, let us start by using a car for an example:

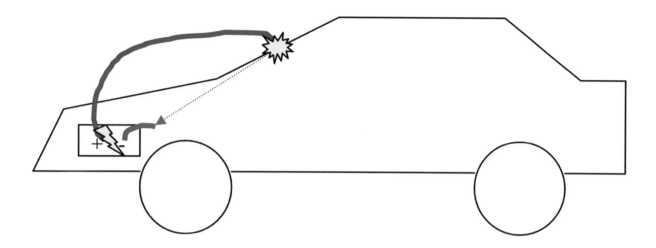

If you were to attach a positive 'jump' lead to a car battery, then accidentally touch the other end of that lead anywhere on the bodywork of the car, you would expect to cause a 'dead short' across the positive and negative of the battery (i.e. a negative 'earth' system)!

'Earthed equipotential bonding and automatic disconnection of supply', uses exactly the same simple principle!

When a 'fused' lead within a low voltage (up to 500v ac), mains Electrical installation comes into contact with any of the exposed metalwork of a building. We should expect to cause a 'dead short' between the 'line circuit conductor' and the 'equipotential bonding conductors' to earth and cause 'automatic disconnection of the supply'.

The 'exposed metalwork' of the building in which an installation is housed, is known either as an 'exposed-conductive-part' or an 'extraneous-conductive-part'.

By connecting extraneous-conductive-parts with the earth terminal of the installation via 'equipotential bonding' conductors (or via 'local supplementary equipotential bonding' and 'circuit protective' conductors), we effectively create a part of a 'loop'. The second part of this 'loop' is the line circuit conductor of a circuit. The 'loop' is then completed if for example, a damaged flexible cable plugged into a socket outlet, then comes into contact with an extraneous-conductive-part.

The term 'loop impedance' is generally used to describe the collective resistance of a circuits' line circuit conductors and 'circuit protective' (earth) conductors only. Our example simply adds two extra elements, the line circuit conductor of the flexible cable and the 'equipotential bonding' (earth) conductors.

As long as the resistance of our 'loop' can be accurately calculated (loop impedance), we can remain in complete control of the speed of the 'automatic disconnection of supply'.

3

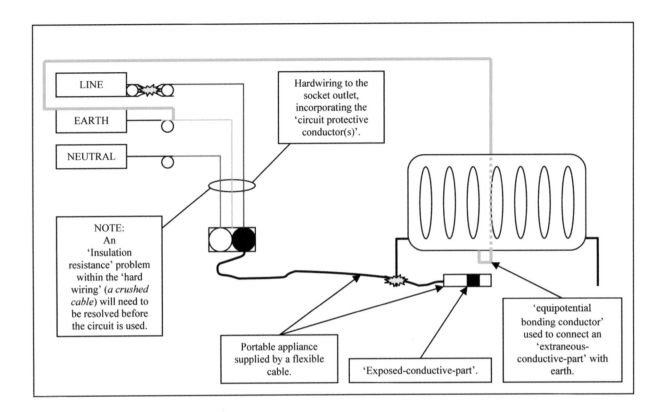

Luckily, a flexible cable is something that is quite difficult to get a firm grip of. If a person should inadvertently pick up a damaged, 'hazardous live' flex, we 'hope' that the flex will be pulled through or out of the hand and as a result, the the contact with the 'hazardous live' part of the flex will be broken.

Therefore we presume that a body coming into contact with a damaged flex will (regardless of the type of protective device used) cause an electric shock of an unknown 'magnitude', but the 'duration' of that shock should not be enough to cause fatalities.

On the other hand if a damaged flex should come into contact with a piece of conductive material (e.g. exposed metalwork), it may unfortunately be possible to firmly grip the piece conductive material, which will inevitably cause the 'duration' of any shock to increase and will therefore significantly increase the likelihood of fatalities!

Therefore when exposed metalwork comes into contact with a 'hazardous live' circuit conductor (in this case our damaged flex), we reduce the 'duration' of any possible resultant shock, by automatically disconnecting the circuit of which the circuit conductor forms a part.

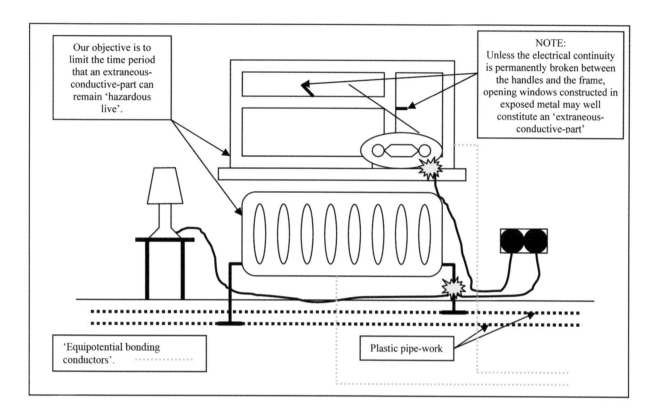

One example of an 'extraneous-conductive-part' would be a 'radiator':

In heating systems which have been entirely installed using copper pipe, the system may be bonded to earth at one point only as the copper pipe-work provides, for our purposes, low resistance electrical continuity between the radiators and the hot water taps (unfortunately the cold water supply is a separate body of water from the heating and hot water, therefore 'equipotential bonding' conductors are used to connect them together and make all of the copper pipe-work as one, this is generally referred to as 'cross bonding').

The majority of 'water' systems now incorporate sections of non-conductive 'plastic pipe work', for our purposes this effectively isolates each radiator (and hot water tap) from any other, creating lots of individual 'extraneous-conductive-parts' instead of just one big one.

To confuse the issue even more the water within the heating and hot water systems (and the cold water system) still provides a 'high resistance' electrical continuity around the systems, effectively linking things together, but providing 'loop impedance' over which we have no control without 'equipotential bonding'.

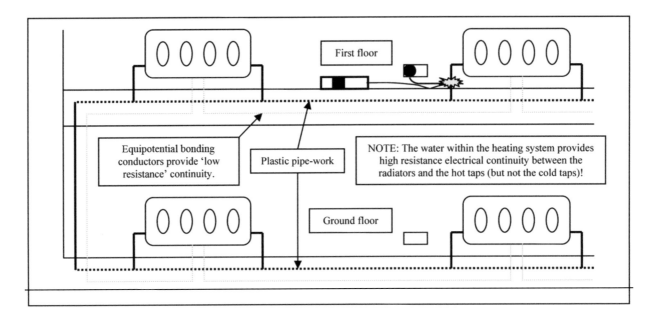

The diagram contains the following labels:

First floor

Equipotential bonding conductors provide 'low resistance' continuity.

Plastic pipe-work

NOTE: The water within the heating system provides high resistance electrical continuity between the radiators and the hot taps (but not the cold taps)!

Ground floor

Any problems that we inherit with the use of flexible, non-conductive water pipes are amplified within a bathroom where the resistance of the human body to electrical current flow, is at its' lowest.

Even where heating and hot and cold water systems are piped entirely in copper. In order to be confident that an earth fault current from somewhere else in the building, does not turn up on one tap in the bathroom, whilst another simultaneously accessible tap or accessory provides an 'earth path', we simply 'cross bond' within the bathroom.

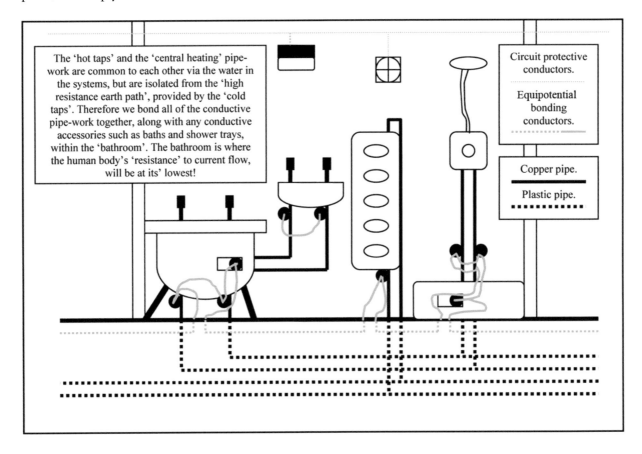

The diagram contains the following labels:

The 'hot taps' and the 'central heating' pipe-work are common to each other via the water in the systems, but are isolated from the 'high resistance earth path', provided by the 'cold taps'. Therefore we bond all of the conductive pipe-work together, along with any conductive accessories such as baths and shower trays, within the 'bathroom'. The bathroom is where the human body's 'resistance' to current flow, will be at its' lowest!

Circuit protective conductors.

Equipotential bonding conductors.

Copper pipe.

Plastic pipe.

In a fully copper piped system, we also employ equipotential bonding sometimes called 'cross bonding' around the hot water tank, usually within an airing cupboard, which is one place where all of the different 'circuits' of pipe-work tend to be present.

Where heating and hot and cold water systems incorporate plastic, non-conductive pipe-work we unfortunately lose the opportunity to 'cross bond' around the hot water tank. This leaves us totally reliant on the 'equipotential bonding/cross bonding' that we employ within the bathroom!

Lighting circuits and other fixed equipment, which may be present within a bathroom, is another subject entirely but has relevance.

All electrical equipment designed to go in a bathroom is either 'IP' rated, or extra low voltage. This means that where these 'high level' circuits are concerned, we intend to 'protect' by relying on insulation and inaccessibility, Rather than earthed equipotential bonding.

If the insulation resistance of a flex should break down whilst the flex is in contact with a radiator or its' associated conductive pipe-work, we must assume that the entire body of water common to that radiator, will carry earth fault current not just to the other radiators, but also the hot taps within the building.
The cold taps within the building will be fed directly from the incoming mains water supply, providing a high resistance electrical path from the cold taps to 'earth'.
Therefore during such fault conditions, a 'potential difference' of 230volts may be introduced between 'simultaneously accessible' hot and cold taps.
Therefore, we simply 'cross bond' them.

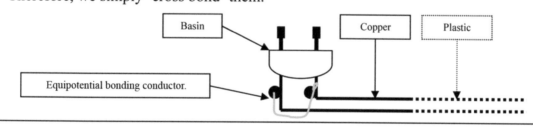

When considering the human body's roll in all of this, thinking in terms of 'series' & 'parallel' may make the subject a little easier to understand:

Our objective can be described as; trying to avoid allowing the human body to come into something we call 'direct contact' with a hazardous live conductor, under fault conditions. This can also be loosely described as, trying to avoid allowing the human body to become a 'series path to earth', under fault conditions.

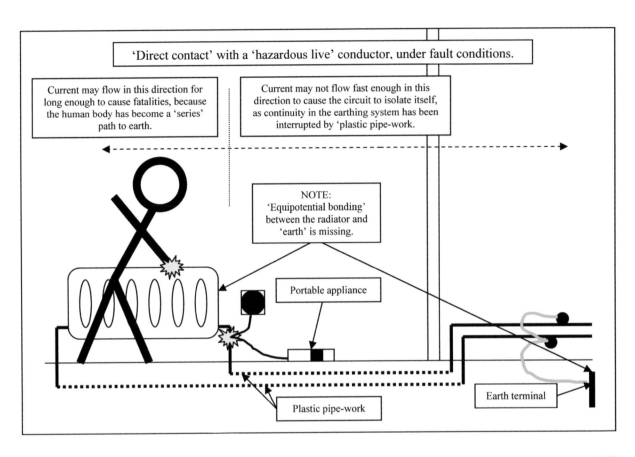

'Direct contact' with a 'hazardous live' conductor, under fault conditions.

Current may flow in this direction for long enough to cause fatalities, because the human body has become a 'series' path to earth.

Current may not flow fast enough in this direction to cause the circuit to isolate itself, as continuity in the earthing system has been interrupted by 'plastic pipe-work.

NOTE:
'Equipotential bonding' between the radiator and 'earth' is missing.

Portable appliance

Plastic pipe-work

Earth terminal

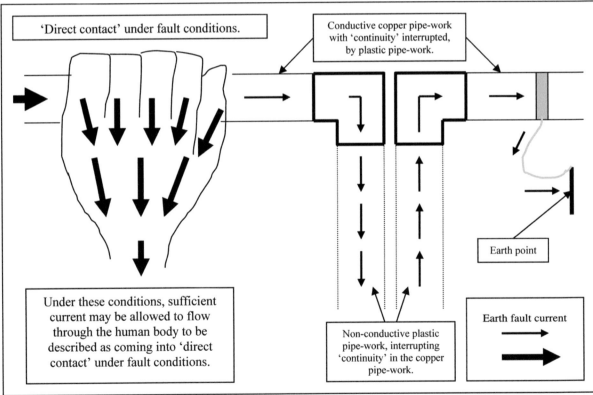

'Direct contact' under fault conditions.

Conductive copper pipe-work with 'continuity' interrupted, by plastic pipe-work.

Under these conditions, sufficient current may be allowed to flow through the human body to be described as coming into 'direct contact' under fault conditions.

Non-conductive plastic pipe-work, interrupting 'continuity' in the copper pipe-work.

Earth point

Earth fault current

Far less current will be allowed to flow through the human body, if the human body is only allowed to come into 'indirect contact' with a hazardous live conductor, under fault conditions. Which can be 'loosely' described as, the human body becoming a secondary *parallel* path to earth', under fault conditions.

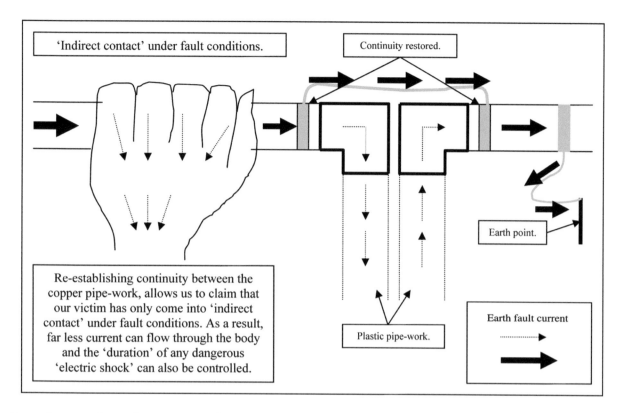

Re-establishing continuity between the copper pipe-work, allows us to claim that our victim has only come into 'indirect contact' under fault conditions. As a result, far less current can flow through the body and the 'duration' of any dangerous 'electric shock' can also be controlled.

In order to reduce the amount of current that can flow through a human body, if it should be in contact with an exposed-conductive/extraneous-conductive-part at the time that a fault occurs; and to ensure that any protective device will disconnect the affected circuit within an appropriate time period, a 'low resistance' conductive path must be established between all exposed-conductive/extraneous-conductive-parts and earth!

Automatic disconnection of supply due to earth fault current, relies with very few exceptions (being in the garden, being one of them) on earthed equipotential bonding in order to function.

The 'residual current device' or the 'residual current circuit breaker with over-current protection', in common with the 'fuse' and the 'miniature circuit breaker', when used as a part of an EEBADS system, relies upon leaking current passing along a low resistance earth path, in order to operate effectively.

The 'RCD' or 'RCBO' reacts primarily to current imbalance, whilst the 'MCB' or 'fuse' reacts to 'overload'. Either reaction is accelerated when the resistance of the earth fault currents' path to earth, is 'low'.

If therefore the human body is stood in a garden on damp grass (which provides a second point of contact, with a low resistance path to earth), when coming into contact with a 'hazardous live' circuit conductor, enough earth fault current should pass through the human body for an RCD/RCBO to disconnect the circuit within 40mS.

If on the other hand the human body is, for example stood inside a house, then our 'neon screwdriver test' would suggest to us, that there is no guarantee that the resistance of our earth path will be low enough, to allow the flow of earth fault current to cause the RCD/RCBO to disconnect the circuit at all!

Note:
Unfortunately if the 'duration' of an electric shock is long enough, a 'magnitude' of far less than 30mA (RCD/RCBO tripping current) of earth fault current, flowing through the human body can be fatal!

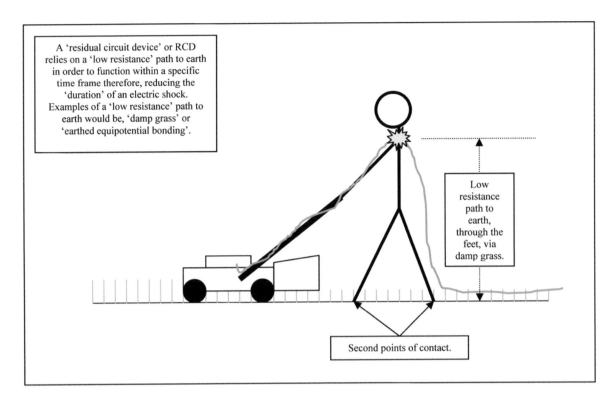

A 'residual circuit device' or RCD relies on a 'low resistance' path to earth in order to function within a specific time frame therefore, reducing the 'duration' of an electric shock. Examples of a 'low resistance' path to earth would be, 'damp grass' or 'earthed equipotential bonding'.

Low resistance path to earth, through the feet, via damp grass.

Second points of contact.

Above I have tried to illustrate an example of the type of situation for which the 'residual current device' and the 'residual current circuit breaker with overload protection', where designed.

In the 'garden', we can accurately predict the resistance through the human body via wet grass to earth, therefore we can be confident of being able to disconnect the circuit with the use of an RCD/RCBO, within a 'duration' of time that will prevent the 'magnitude' of current being fatal, when the 'potential difference' is 230volts ac.

A 'residual circuit device' or RCD will certainly allow up to 30mA of leaking current to flow through the human body. Unfortunately given a long enough 'duration' of time, far less than a 30mA 'magnitude' of current can be fatal.
As this example shows. What will inevitably be a 'high resistance' path to earth inside a building, will leave us reliant on the flex being pulled through the grasp of the hand, in order to 'break' this 'direct contact' with a 'hazardous live' circuit conductor.

The resistance of this earth path will be a 'constant variable'. Therefore we cannot accurately predict our 'loop impedance', or disconnection time.

Above I have tried to illustrate an example where an RCD/RCBO 'alone', cannot be relied upon to disconnect the circuit. Here we are still reliant on the flex being pulled through, or out of the hand, in order to break 'direct contact' with a 'hazardous live' circuit conductor.

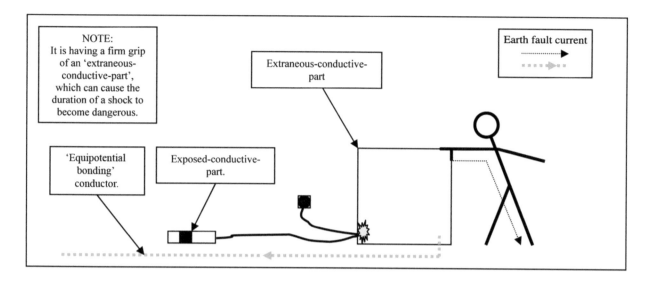

Above I have tried to illustrate the most common problem concerning large or otherwise immovable, conductive parts of a building (extraneous-conductive-parts).

Our priority under this type of fault condition is to disconnect the circuit before any serious injury can occur.

If we think back to our 'neon screwdriver' for a moment, we will remember that the fault path through the human body to earth is a 'constant variable'. Therefore there is no guarantee that under these conditions, an RCD/RCBO will disconnect the circuit un-aided.

We are left with no alternative, but to return the vast majority of earth fault current to 'earth' via equipotential bonding conductors, from the extraneous-conductive-part to the earth terminal of the installation.

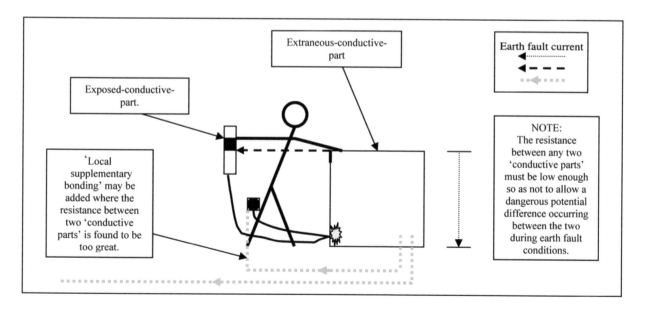

Above I have tried to illustrate an example of 'simultaneous contact with simultaneously accessible earthed conductive parts under fault conditions'.

As in the example above the lower resistance path to earth through the human body will almost certainly be across the 'heart' (attracted by the exposed-conductive-part of the portable appliance), this type of occurrence can be very dangerous unless the resistance between the two earthed conductive parts is low enough to prevent a dangerous potential difference occurring between the two. Another of the objectives of an EEBADS system is to ensure that the resistance between any simultaneously accessible conductive parts (any of which could reasonably foresee-ably become 'hazardous live') is low enough so as not to allow any dangerous potential differences occurring between them during fault conditions. *Where the resistance between simultaneously accessible conductive parts (or the earth terminal of a socket outlet capable of supplying portable equipment with exposed-conductive-parts) is found to be too high, 'local supplementary equipotential bonding' conductors are used to connect the simultaneously accessible conductive parts (or the accessible conductive parts and the earth terminal of the socket outlet) together, effectively reducing the resistance between them to an acceptable level.*

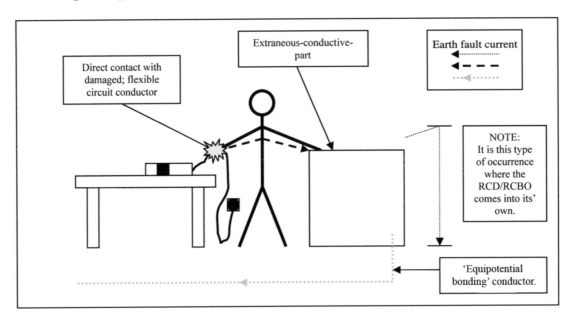

Above I have tried to illustrate an example of 'contact with an earthed conductive part whilst being simultaneously in contact with a damaged, energized line circuit conductor'.

As once more the lower resistance path to earth through the human body will almost certainly be across the 'heart' (in this example attracted by the extraneous-conductive-part), this type of occurrence can be very dangerous if the circuit is only protected by a 'fuse' or an 'MCB'. It is this type of occurrence, where there is a second point of contact is with an 'earthed conductive part' that will potentially allow huge amounts of current to flow 'across' the human 'heart', where the use of an RCD/RCBO indoors comes into its' own, restricting the flow of current to a maximum of 30mA and automatically disconnecting the supply within a maximum of 40mS.

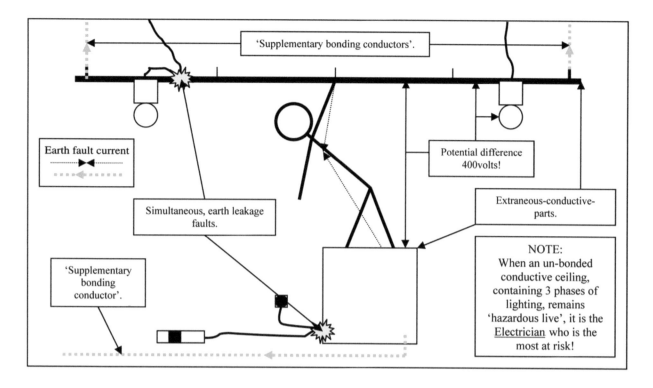

Above I have tried to illustrate 'indirect contact under fault conditions' with two 'simultaneous faults'.

The 'objective' here can only presently be, to minimise this type of occurrence by disconnecting the circuits before the human body gets involved (an objective that can only successfully be achieved by returning earth fault current to the earth terminal of the installation, via 'supplementary bonding conductors').

It may be rare, but even when both 'extraneous-conductive-parts' are recognised as such and 'earth bonded' accordingly. If a human body is in such a position, when the two faults occur simultaneously (in this example, within a maximum of 5seconds of each other), it is almost certain to be fatal.

This is because our protection equipment is all designed around a potential difference of 230volts; here we could well be dealing with a potential difference of 400volts!

Therefore where multi phase supplies are involved, 'earthed equipotential bonding' is currently the only form of protection against phase too phase (400volt) simultaneous contact, under multiple fault conditions!

This is obviously also of relevance in the dry conditions of Australia or Southern Europe.

Summary:
The intention of earthed equipotential bonding therefore is, to create a situation where all of the conductive parts within an installation that could present a danger if they were to become 'hazardous live' as a result of having come into contact with an energized circuit conductor, are connected to

the main earthing point of the installation by conductors of a sufficient size and current carrying capacity so as to automatically disconnect the supply within a specified time when a fault to earth occurs.

Whether the accessible conductive part is of a portable appliance (exposed) or of a building (extraneous) if it can conceivably cause the duration of an electric shock to be increased because once is in the grip of the human hand it may not be 'let go' under earth fault conditions, circuit protective (exposed) and/or local supplementary bonding/supplementary bonding (extraneous) conductors must be in place to return 'earth fault current' to the main earthing point of the building so that automatic disconnection of supply can be induced and the danger can be averted.

It is also important to note that care must be taken to ensure that no dangerous potential differences (voltages/touch voltages) can occur between simultaneously accessible earthed conductive parts, so as not to risk earthed conductors themselves presenting a danger during earth fault conditions. Simply reducing the resistances between simultaneously accessible earthed conductive parts, or between earthed conductive parts and the earth terminals of general purpose socket-outlets likely to supply portable appliances with exposed-conductive-parts which could become simultaneously accessible, can ensure this.

The recent addition of the RCD/RCBO used in conjunction with EEBADS can have the affect of 'fine tuning' this area of Electrical Safety, reducing the dangers associated with a victim coming into contact with an energized circuit conductor whilst simultaneously being in contact with an earthed conductive part!

In conclusion:
It is the Electricians' job to decide what constitutes an 'extraneous-conductive-part'.

Flexes and extension leads will get damaged (e.g. repeated vacuuming with the vacuum cleaner plugged into the same socket outlet, will cause the lead to come into contact with the same objects, at the same points along its' length, time after time. If the object is a wrought iron newel post, we can liven up the entire staircase if we're not careful!).

For as long as we use 'conductive' construction materials, such materials must be insulated, inaccessible or bonded to earth!

About the Author

David Cockburn is an Electrician who was given a start in the industry by his Father.

Nearly a decade and a half of practical experience preceded a highly successful college education, followed by a promising individual career in Electrical Installation.

Latterly David has spent his time educating himself in the field of British and European Electrical and Fire Alarm Installation Safety Standards.

Printed in the United States
By Bookmasters